A Letter to My Daughters

Be the Best You!

Doyin Olorunfemi

ISBN-13: **978-1542792820**
ISBN-10: **1542792827**

Table of Contents

Acknowledgments

Tamilore and Damisi, what a privilege it is to be your mum. I have enjoyed every moment of the journey so far and know that the words in this book will help you live to your full potential if you heed them.

To my dear husband, Kayode, thank you for encouraging me to persist with following my dreams and showing the world my heart through the Minute Motivation videos. Together we are impacting our world!

To my dear friend Tonye Adenusi, thank you for proofreading this book and giving such valuable feedback as I wrote.

To Flo Falayi, thank you for cowriting Part 3 – fatherly advice written from the heart.

To Ade Ajetunmobi, thank you for creating such a beautiful cover.

To my late dad, Aderemi Ade-Ayeni, and my loving mum, Remilekun Ayeni, thank you for instilling in me the discipline of hard work.

To my siblings, Deniyi, Kemi, Tunji, Nike, and Bola - those nights spent chatting away in Navy

Town are some of my fondest memories. Thank you for creating them.

To all my friends who cheer me on, this is for *your* daughters, too.

And, most importantly, to you my Lord and Saviour, thank you for always being so near, flooding my mind with ideas, and giving me the strength to go on. Indeed, in you I live, move, and have my being.

Preface

My dear daughter,

It started with a reflection. What makes me successful, and what can I share with you from my past to make *you* successful for the rest of your life? My mentors? The books I've read? The friends I have? There's so much I can point to.

This is why today I made the decision to write you this letter that will serve as a reminder of my path to success and provide a road map for you to enjoy success beyond that which I have.

At first I considered taking you on a road trip, but that would not have allowed me to pass the baton on properly, for my story is not just for you, but for your friends and your daughters, too.

Besides, I might have left out a few important points and lost the accuracy that is needed in a story that I believe will shape your future.

In Part 2, I have left spaces for you to write as you reflect on the thoughts I share. I therefore recommend you read this letter with a pen in hand. I believe writing will help you consolidate your learning.

This letter is written to encourage, inspire, and point you to the realities that are a part of life and shine a torch of hope where there is uncertainty. It is my sincere desire that you will **learn** from my journey, **adopt** the attitudes that shaped me, **understand** the effect of relationships, and **apply** the truth from my acronyms.

PART 1

My Journey

My Journey

I will become a plant; it's my decision, and it's my choice.

Who am I? Why am I alive? Am I living as the best version of me? These are questions I ask myself periodically. The experiences in my past make me know there's a reason I'm alive today. I know I am special and that I have unique strengths and gifts that influence my world positively. I live every day with intent, and, more than anything, I desire to go to bed daily thinking, "I did the best I could with today, and I maximised my potential!"

Lately I have been fascinated by that word, *potential* - so much so that it's become one of my favourites. *Potential* sums up the resident ability of an item. It connotes the strength that can be but may not have been discovered yet; it celebrates the uniqueness that makes an object (or a person) achieve greatness. It can transform as much as it can weigh down, and its end result will be determined by the decision to tap into and maximise it.

I strongly believe that every single person walking on the planet is an embodiment of promise, possessing a unique quality that makes him or her different from everyone else. However, our potential to be great comes in an untapped form and needs to undergo a process to help it come to life. In my short time here on earth, I have seen many people live with heavy hearts because of the weight of the potential they carry, a potential they have never had the opportunity to birth . That's what I mean by *"potential can weigh you down."* On the other hand, I have also had the privilege of seeing people transformed, growing into powerhouses of change for themselves and those in their world—this is what I mean by *"potential can transform."*

As your mother, I want you to live to the fullness of your potential and to be great; I want you to achieve all that you were put on earth to do. In this chapter I will share with you a big chunk of my story. Hopefully you will see how I began my journey to maximising my potential and how I chose to allow potential to transform me rather than weigh me down.

You've probably seen seeds that grow to become plants. Every seed has the ability to become a thriving plant that benefits those around it. Unfortunately, not all seeds achieve this. I think that human life is much like the journey of a seed, and just as a seed that maximises its potential will become a plant, you can become the best version of you. Let me illustrate with a story.

There was a seed that had been stuck in a bag for a long time. One day, someone opened up the bag and put the seed in some soil, and while the seed was excited to be out of the bag, she soon began to think, "Hey, I'm alone here. What happened to all my friends? Why aren't they coming along?"

She was lonely, and soon her questions turned to frustration, which turned to confusion and then despair. This weighed down the seed.

In spite of this, the little seed began to think that being in the soil perhaps felt a bit more natural than being in that bag of comfort.

"Could this be a better place for me?" She considered, as despair slowly gave way to hope, allowing the seed to start exploring the possibilities presented by this new location. She soon accepted her new home and chose to make the most of it, making the adjustments necessary for her to thrive in her new environment. As she did so, she found that she began to change ever so slowly. Her hard, shiny outer shell got softer, and pretty soon it started to split open. She noticed that she started to become a bit smelly and wondered if it was due to her new home, which was dark and damp. Although she wondered, she didn't worry; somehow she felt that things were meant to be this way, despite the decay and sure death she felt were coming to her.

What our precious seed didn't realise was that much the same way a caterpillar changes into a butterfly, she was also going through a change. And one day she woke up to find that she was alive and different! She was no longer the tiny little speck that lived in a comfortable pack: she was on her way to becoming. She found herself growing in ways she'd never thought possible, and very soon she broke through the soil. She realised that she had changed from seed to plant. No longer an insignificant little speck, she was something of significance to be loved, appreciated, and enjoyed.

Time passed, and she settled into this new role, but one day she woke up feeling unwell. Something had changed her course of growth. It felt as if a foreign object had attacked her. The word, had the plant been able to speak, was *pests*. These pests seemed to have only one aim – destruction - and, boy, were they determined!

Soon the leaves of the plant, once a healthy shade of green, looked withered and shrivelled. For the first time in a long time, she no longer wanted to be a plant. She craved the seed pack she had come from. "Perhaps this journey was not one to take. Perhaps this is the end of a beginning that should never have been," she thought. Slowly her questions turned to frustration, which turned to confusion and then despair. This weighed down the seed.

By this time, our little seed was good and ready to give up, but just in time someone intercepted. She felt what seemed to be sprinkles of water — stinging at first but then refreshing. The smell was strong and uncomfortable, but the itch left by the pests was soothed. Slowly the plant began to feel better, and once again she prepared to continue her journey, becoming a plant that would benefit all around her. Only this time she was going to be careful.

Careful? What was that all about? Did *careful* mean limiting the influences around her - not allowing herself to be touched without restraint by the sun that gives light or the moisture that comes from the soil to strengthen her? Did *careful* mean second-guessing everyone and interpreting every event with the stained eyes of past hurts? Somehow, the plant had become very fearful, timid, and unsure. She questioned, rationalised against, and pulled away from the very sources of her strength because of the fear of the pests attacking again. Unfortunately, as she protected herself, she began to look quite unsightly: her leaves became dull and droopy as she once again fell back into the cycle of questions turning to frustration, confusion, and despair, which weighed her down.

"Perhaps the sprinkler will appear and make it all better again," the plant thought. She hoped and waited, still believing in the miracle of days gone past, but nothing of the kind was in sight.

One day she realised that what was destroying her this time was coming from within. It was fear that was preventing her from accepting the nourishment that helped her grow. Unlike before, this had nothing to do with any external force; this was an internal sabotage. The plant knew that a decision had to be made; she knew death would be the only result if she didn't make a choice - and soon.

With brokenness and an iota of faith, she yielded to what was natural to her. Once again she allowed in the sun and the moisture from the soil. Within a short time, she began to grow again, once again becoming all she could and should be. Once again her leaves became green and strong; once again they looked fresh and well nurtured, and all who went by could see that she had returned to being a picture of her true self.

If you read that journey and for a moment identified with the seed becoming a healthy plant, perhaps you will identify with my story.

Being the third out of six children born to my parents, I always felt that I was special. My reasons for believing this may not have made sense to anyone else, but I embraced them as true and definitive. I remember conducting a random poll among my friends and trying to convince them that there was something special about me. My reason? I was the only one who had an older brother, older sister, younger brother, and younger sisters.

I also felt I was special because there were eight years between me and my oldest and youngest siblings. I was right in the middle—perfection! It makes me smile to remember, but as a ten-year-old, I was sure I could take on the world. I believed everything around my birth, positioning, and equipping was a sign from God of just how special I was.

Feeling special may really have been the fuel that helped me go through school as a model student. I never got into any trouble that made my parents cringe, and I rewarded their faith in me with academic excellence. I excelled at every exam I took and got into the schools I chose to go to. I also found my faith and committed to a relationship with Jesus Christ at the age of ten. This public proclamation of faith meant that even though I was all on my own in boarding school, I had a grounding and deferred my decision making to what I believed and understood from my Bible—a most treasured companion.

While at the university studying Computer Engineering, I met and fell in love with Kayode. He was, and still is, my best friend. We would stay up for hours on end and just dream, talk, and boost each other up. Time stood still when we were together; nothing mattered but the love we shared and professed. He didn't have much, but all he had, I could have. He lavished me with words and gifts, and I knew I was the queen of his heart. It was little wonder I couldn't wait to be married to him. I knew nothing would make me happier.

Two years into our courtship, he moved to the United Kingdom. I think those were some of the toughest days of my life. We soon decided we didn't want to spend any more days apart, so we picked our wedding date—February 19, 2000. We were determined to make it the best day ever. Preparations went into full swing, and on February 12, exactly a week before our wedding, Kayode arrived at Murtala Muhammed Airport, Lagos, where I was waiting to greet him. Our reunion was joyful, marred only by the news that his luggage had been left behind in the United Kingdom and had to be picked up the following day.

"Well," we thought, "we have six days to sort it out," and we left for home.

The following day was Sunday, so after church and a meal with some friends, we headed back to the airport to pick up his luggage. Thankfully it had arrived, and we were able to take his things home. Unfortunately, the luggage was not all we took home. Tailing us were three hoodlums—armed robbers, as we would later find out. They followed us in and stripped us of everything we had: they took our money, our rings, and even Kayode's wedding shoes.

That experience stole my confidence. I struggled to trust God. I began to feel that I always needed to watch my back, and I had constant nightmares. Fear had truly been imprinted in the core of my being.

Think back to the seed in my previous illustration. I once was secure and confident in my family life, with siblings who cared and parents who did the best they could for me. The bond between us kept me comfortable and secure; however, as I grew older, that comfort was shelved, and I was put in the world to find my feet. And find my feet I did: I did well for myself; I prospered in everything I set out to do. I was a truly blossoming plant! Even now I remember leaving the university and having one of the best jobs of my classmates. Favour literally pursued me everywhere. I found favour in ways I couldn't have fathomed. I was a thriving plant, and everyone around me saw it and benefited from it.

The armed robbery and all that came with it was the pest, a parasite that lived in me. It came upon me without warning at what should have been the happiest time of my life.

Yet more pests have been picked up along the way, which I will not bore you with in this book. What is important for you to know is that it took fourteen whole years for me to allow the sprinklers to heal me from the damaging effects of those pests. Once confident, I became shy and withdrawn. I sometimes sought work as a distraction; I made friends, but I didn't trust them enough to allow them to get too close. My zeal for life definitely took a hit; no longer was I keen on taking on the world. To be safe was enough for me, and I shelved the excitement of dreaming and seeking to be the best me. In other words, *I settled.*

So how did it all change? Well, I found my sprinkling as I approached my fortieth birthday. Even though I was successful, I knew something was missing. I wasn't the person I had started out as. I wanted to be that girl who was on course to take on the world, so I set out on a journey of discovery. With an outlandish year planned, I was sure to rediscover me.

As I celebrated with a different event every month, I encountered another sprinkle that would deliver me from my pests. On November 9, 2014, I heard the news of the death of Dr. Myles Munroe. Like many people around the world, I was shaken by the news. However, I remembered. I remembered growing up on his books in my days at the university, long before the pests attacked. In particular, I remembered reading the book *In Pursuit of Purpose*, and realised that this time I was ready for that book.

For two days after his death, I scoured the Internet for materials of his and spent hours listening to his teachings. I felt a commission that week and decided it was time to shelve the pests and go for growth again.

In December 2014, I stepped out with my *Minute Motivation* video series and blog. To say I was surprised by the public's reception would be putting it mildly. The weekly broadcasts started, and as I spoke, I was freed. Life started revealing new meaning. Suddenly I didn't feel the need to be defined by the things around me. What mattered was that every day I did my very best to improve the world and help make those around me the best versions of themselves.

You see, my dear daughter, you grow as you help others grow. My fortieth-year celebration allowed me to dream again, and my YouTube channel (*Minute Motivation with Doyin*) and the ability to help others gave me a purpose and reason to thrive. I began to remember that I, by my choices, can make the world a better place.

Of course, reconnecting with my vision and pursuing it came with challenges. I had to develop the skills that would keep my vision alive and thriving, and this meant making sacrifices in other areas. I reduced the number of hours I gave to my business and suffered financially as a result, but I understood that to have an impact, one must be willing to sometimes lose ground in order to gain even more ground.

There is a time for tilling the ground and planting the seeds. And while there is frustration in not seeing the physical reality of these sacrifices, there is also the excitement of seeing new life revealed. Then there is the discipline needed to maintain that growth, and finally there is the need to gain knowledge so that the growth can reach its full potential. This cycle is one I have come to understand and embrace. I have learnt to identify which stage I'm in at any point in time and do my bit to enjoy the season and advance in it.

Essentially, I rediscovered my purpose. I realised that the only way to keep my dream alive was to subject myself to intense nurturing. I found the shortcut in books—the more I read, the more enlightened I became, and the less fearful I was of sabotaging myself or seeing my dream implode

I launched 'Let's Read', as an offshoot of *Minute Motivation* in January 2016, and today I am living as that thriving plant again.

When I look back now at the most destructive pest—the armed robbery in February 2000—I realise that the reason I wasn't killed that day (despite the fact that the hoodlums had guns) is that my message was being preserved to benefit someone else. I know that as a farmer instructs others how to maximise the potential in their seed, I have to teach you how to fight your pests and subject yourself to nurturing so that you can grow to your fullest extent.

Dear daughter, realise that as you grow in life, you will have your own experiences. I pray to God that when you do, you will have enough knowledge and understanding to shake off negative experiences and move on from them more quickly than I did by remembering these three nuggets of wisdom:

1. Negative experiences are not meant to kill you, but to strengthen and validate you for the task you have been assigned.

2. You determine how long you permit those experiences to steal from you. Address them quickly and move on to your purpose.

3. As long as you stay grounded, you are sure to pull through.

In the next chapter, I describe how, even in my pest-infested season, I found strength and developed character. I have titled it "These Attitudes." The attitudes discussed will set you apart and point you towards being the best version of yourself.

You must decide if you are going to rob the world or bless it with the rich, valuable, potent, untapped resources locked away within you"

—Dr Myles Munroe

PART 2

These Attitudes

These Attitudes

I will always be the best version of me.

I smile as I remember the first time I sent you a text at two o'clock in the morning. You had forgotten to put your phone on silent mode, and the beeping woke you up. You scolded me and pointed me to the scheduling feature. I have since learnt to use that feature, and now when I wake up at four in the morning—as I love to do—I can type out all my messages and not wake the recipients up in the process: I simply schedule them.

You realise, don't you, that nothing changed in the phone except that I became aware of a new capability, a new potential, and found a way to use my phone in such a way that it maximised that potential, caused minimal discomfort, and achieved my goals. This chapter is the same.

Reading my story might have sparked ideas in you, and you may well be ready to take the first step to rid yourself of your parasites, find your nurturing, and maximise your potential, but I want you to do it in such a way that your message does not cause anyone discomfort. I want you to maximise your potential knowing the right tools and using them wisely.

Throughout this chapter, I have written out the attitudes that helped me to become who I am today. To help you remember, I have written them out the way I taught you to read—from *A* to *Z*. At the end of each letter, take some time to ponder the questions that follow. Put a tick next to those you have mastered and an asterisk next to those you want to come back to. If you are unsure how well you have mastered a particular attitude, ask a close friend. A true friend will be honest in letting you know what to work on!

Attitude is a choice. Happiness is a choice. Optimism is a choice. Kindness is a choice. Giving is a choice. Respect is a choice. Whatever choice you make makes you. Choose wisely.

—Roy T. Bennett

A Is for *Affirmation*

It is sad that most people notice your flaws before they see your worth. As a woman, especially, much of your life will likely be spent subconsciously trying to live up to an expectation: being a good wife or a competent mother, dressing fashionably or fitting into the right size—it just never stops.

Can I encourage you, my dear? In the midst of all of these, find the strength to seek out what is great about you. One of the most powerful things I have learnt is the power of affirmation—the act of talking about yourself positively until you believe and then become what you're saying. While I know you have flaws, I know you have strengths, too! Who you eventually become, however, is dependent on what you focus on. Choose to wake up daily and confess your strengths. For instance, I say this to myself: "I am Dynamic, Organized, Youthful, Influential, and Nice." They are positive adjectives that spell out my name, one for each letter.

This was how I first learnt to affirm myself—a simple yet effective way. Since then, I have added more adjectives and built up my affirmation, and now I run through positive statements, incorporating positive adjectives and spoken to myself naturally. Most of these statements are now evident in my life; and others are still a work in progress.

Remember, machinery needs oil to keep it working smoothly, and so do you! Your positive words lubricate the machinery that is your dream and help it to reach success.

Take Action

1. Do you have an affirmation? Yes/No
2. Write out your name in the box below, vertically and for each letter, choose an adjective that you would want to describe you.

3. Take a picture of the box with your phone, and let it be the first thing you look at and the first words you speak to

yourself every day. Say the words until you believe and become them.

4. Write positive, impactful statements incorporating these adjectives, and build a daily statement "chant" that affirms you and builds you up. For instance – "I am confident, knowledgeable, wise, hardworking and successful in all I do". Can you imagine the energy you will have all day if you said this to yourself first thing in the morning?

It's one thing to stop saying the wrong things, but you've got to start saying the right things.

—Joyce Meyer

B Is for *Belief*

Everyone believes in something. Believing in something or someone bigger than you helps you make sense of instances in your life that would normally defy meaning. Think about positive outcomes that came from situations you had totally given up on. These had to have been the result of someone bigger than you.

In the last chapter, I described how my Christian faith shaped my early life and how it kept me focused and sane in my dark times. If it were not for my faith in God and the constant warmth of His presence when I was desolate, I would not be here today. Take time to understand who you are, what you believe, and why you believe it. Then wholly devote yourself to that belief. Be committed to growing in it. I assure you that it will be the anchor that holds you and provides perspective when life seems grim and unbearable.

Life cannot be lived from a position of myopia that assumes everything is all about us and the limited realm in which we live. I believe there definitely is God out there, and trusting Him brings strength to our minute world.

Take Action

1. Write down one instance when you had unexplainable positive outcome in a situation you had given up on.

   _____

   _____

   _____

2. How would you explain the results you got?

   _____

   _____

   _____

If you don't stand for something you will fall for anything.

—Gordon A. Eadie

C Is for *Communication*

Be heard! Say what you want to say, and ensure there's never a reason for ambiguity. Understand that communication is an art that weaves your words with body language and the tone of your voice.

First, words. I suggest you become a wordsmith. A woman with a rich vocabulary will stand out among the many mutterings that have become the order of today. If you make the choice to learn a new word every day and use it as often as you can until you have full grasp of it, by the time you're old and grey, you will know almost every word that exists. What respect this will earn you, as people will be dazzled by your wealth of words!

Always colour your rich words with a smile, for listeners will be enveloped by the warmth of your smile as you speak the words that enrich them.

Lastly, be sure to connect with your listener. After all, what use are words when your listener feels they are not directed at her? Look her in the eyes, find the spot on her face that touches her soul, and you will reach her heart—not just her head—with your words.

Take Action

1. Do you communicate well? Yes/No
2. What do you do well?

   _____

   _____

   _____

3. What do you need to work on?

   _____

   _____

   _____

4. What is your plan for communicating better?

   _____

   _____

   _____

In communication, words account for 7%, tone of voice accounts for 38%, and body language accounts for 55% of the liking. They are often abbreviated as the "3 Vs" for Verbal, Vocal & Visual.

—from the studies of Albert Mehrabian

D Is for *Driven*

Don't stop, don't quit, and don't ever give up! What are you passionate about? What pulls at your heartstrings? When you find it, be totally committed to it. Speak about it with enthusiasm, and allow your commitment to it energise your world.

I sincerely believe that it's your choice to be driven or demotivated. I have intentionally contrasted those words because I want you to understand that the flip side of being driven is to lose motivation. If you don't allow your passion to dictate your daily actions such that you begin to see growth, frustration will eat away at you and cause you to shrivel. I hope you choose the path of growth and wake up daily with the desire to become better. Embrace the challenges that come your way, and allow them to propel you to greater heights. Decide that nothing will stop you and that everything will enhance you.

And when you lay your head to rest at night, dream of a tomorrow that is better than today. As long as you keep aiming higher than your best, you will have the drive to take on the world and live fully.

Take Action

1. How old are you? _____
2. Subtract your age from 75, and multiply the result by 2. (For example, if you are 20, your response here would be 110.)
   _____
3. Using your response to the question above as X, write a list of X things you want to achieve—places you want to visit, the salary you hope to earn, and so on. Just dream!
4. Make the most of every opportunity to achieve the items your list.

Don't limit yourself. Many people limit themselves to what they think they can do. You can go as far as your mind lets you. What you believe, remember, you can achieve.

—Mary Kay Ash

E Is for *Excellence*

When you finish a task, do you look back and give yourself a thumbs up, or do you wish you had done a bit more? The decision to be excellent is one I pray you embrace. Be determined to give your very best, and in doing so you will be measured as the best among the rest. If you learn the skills that you need and refuse to settle for mediocrity, soon others will speak about you.

I give my best to everything, from putting the dishes in the cabinet to aiming for a first-class degree. The task doesn't matter. I have learnt that the decision to extol excellence is in the mind, and you need to practice it daily. So let me encourage you to make the best of even small tasks. If you do, making the bigger tasks excellent will become second nature to you. Once you master this, people will talk about you, and your name will be the first when recommendations are needed. I know this because it accounts for the success I've had in business. The referrals never stop coming, and business is stronger daily because my customers trust me to give my very best!

Take Action

1. List three activities you are engaged in at the moment.

   _____

   _____

   _____

   _____

2. How can you do them better?

   _____

   _____

   _____

   _____

Be a yardstick of quality. Some people aren't used to an environment where excellence is expected.

— Steve Jobs

F Is for *Fun*

Life can be hard, and too many people are grumpy and unhappy. Choose not to become Ms. Grumpy! In my bid not to be dull and boring, I found myself focusing on the dull and the boring. You can guess what my results were. Yes, I became even more dull and boring!

As I get older, I realise that the way to not be grumpy is to find an antidote, and the best antidote I've found is fun. I work hard to put myself in a happy place and have fun at every opportunity. Apart from the magnetic effect this has on the people around me, being a fun person gives me energy that keeps me from tiring; there's always that extra reserve. To develop your fun factor, do the following:

1. Wake up daily with a smile.
2. Don't be too hard on yourself. Laugh a lot, and don't be afraid to look silly.
3. Plan times of relaxation, and do what you enjoy.
4. Celebrate people around you and ensure that they smile when you're around them.

It's good to have fun, so enjoy the strength it gives.

Take Action

1. Plan a fun outing with three of your closest friends. Below are some examples of things to do:
    a. Go to the movies.
    b. Enjoy a day at the spa.
    c. Have a picnic on the beach.
2. Ensure that your outing is guided by a budget and that everyone has a belly laugh.

Don't live life so seriously, always have time to laugh! Laughter not only adds years to your life, but adds life to your years!!!

Anonymous

G Is for *Goals*

Have you ever tried going somewhere without knowing where you were headed? Few things in life are as frustrating as living daily without a sense of direction. Having a goal means you know where you are headed, and it provides room for you to change direction, if need be, on this journey of life.

There are many formulae for setting goals, but my recommendation is to take time and understand your purpose before setting any goals. Knowing your purpose is the fuel that feeds the flame of achievement when it seems to be burning out.

Once you understand your reason, you need to make the goal as SMART as you can. SMART is an acronym: Specific, Measurable, Action-focused, Realistic, and Timed. An example of a smart goal is, "I will learn how to cycle confidently enough to cycle on the road by July 31, 2017." All the elements of being SMART are incorporated in that goal.

I have heard it said before that a good goal must be realistic and have a 50 percent chance of happening. In other words, if I have never been on a bicycle, I shouldn't set a goal to cycle confidently on the road in two days.

After setting your goal, take time to break it down into the smallest steps. From my experience, I can tell you that once I get to the point where the steps look achievable, I am able to apply the necessary discipline to bring my goals to fruition. Big goals that are not broken into plans remain abstract and are thus less likely to be accomplished.

Be bold enough to set your yearly goal, but be wise enough to break it down into monthly, weekly, and daily goals. The discipline of living today well is what guarantees a successful tomorrow.

Take Action

1. Go back to the list you created in "*D* Is for *Driven*" above, and write out those things you want to achieve this year.
2. Create a SMART goal from at least three of them. The goal could be a step that helps you achieve the dream. For example, if you wrote that you want to study law in Cambridge, your goal this year might be to get 85 percent or more on all history tests this year.
3. Make a poster that states the goal and displays a picture representing it, and then hang the poster some place where you'll see it daily.

Our goals can only be reached through a vehicle of a plan, in which we must fervently believe, and upon which we must vigorously act. There is no other route to success.

—Stephen A. Brennan

H Is for *Health*

I smile as I write this section because health is still a work in progress for me. I know I should be concerned about my health—it is the one thing that could stop me in my tracks as I work towards being the best me—but I find myself succumbing to the lure of ice cream and rich puddings.

Is health just about food? Certainly not! A healthy lifestyle depends on a combination of what you put into your body and how you keep your body. Two important goals in this area are to only allow into your body what it needs and to exercise well enough that your body reaches its optimum stretch.

At times in my life I was trim and even admired by others for having a fab body shape even though I knew I was unhealthy—I could hardly navigate a flight of stairs without panting. On the other hand, I have seen those with a more generous body size tackle physical activities that I wouldn't dare try. My words to you today are *get the balance right*. Balance your plate by ensuring all the right nutrients are in place, and then commit to thirty minutes of moderate exercise daily. Your body will thank you and serve you longer.

Take Action

1. What improvement can you make to your diet this week? Write "nothing" if you're doing great.

   _____

   _____

2. How and when will you exercise this week?

   _____

   _____

A fit, healthy body—that is the best fashion statement.

—Jess C. Scott

I Is for *Invest*

I am not a financial expert, but I do know a thing or two about keeping some of today's bounty for tomorrow. For one, living today with tomorrow in mind keeps you calm and well equipped to face tomorrow. I have been self-employed for fourteen years, which means that some months are exceptional and others are quiet. There's therefore always a need for me to balance out my lifestyle so I don't expend too much in the bountiful times.

Luckily for me, I read *The Richest Man in Babylon* two years into being self-employed and made a decision to spend a maximum of 70 percent of my earnings: 10 percent went to the church as a tithe, 10 percent went to my savings (to accommodate the washing machine breaking down and the like), and 10 percent I put into investment funds that will mature when I am fifty and older. What seemed like a simple decision at the time is one of the reasons I smile so confidently at the future. While not all the investments have done as well as I would have liked, this method of investing keeps me disciplined and gives me something to look forward to.

I highly recommend you read that book and come up with your own plan for investing, saving, and spending before you come into the wealth I believe befits you. What you invest doesn't have to be a lot; it just has to be consistent. As the old adage says, "Little drops of water make a mighty ocean." If you ever need advice on investing, pay the best advisers so that your losses, if any, will be minimal.

Take Action

1. Make a monthly budget on 70 percent of your income.
2. Open two extra accounts, one for investments and one for savings. Be disciplined in your saving and investing for the next twelve months.
3. Make a commitment to learn about money and how it works. Below are some suggested books:
   a. *Think and Grow Rich* by Napoleon Hill
   b. *The Richest Man in Babylon* by George Clason
   c. *The Science of Getting Rich* by Wallace D. Wattles

If you wish to get rich, save what you get. A fool can earn money; but it takes a wise man to save and dispose of it to his own advantage.

—Brigham Young

J Is for *Journal*

As you get older, you will learn a lot—from books, from people, and from circumstances in life. I encourage you to capture these experiences in a journal.

Understanding the power of a journal was something that I learned later in life, and I dare say that writing in a journal is one of the most exhilarating things I do. I have found my journal to be my best friend—one I can talk to without being judged and one I can be sure will keep my confidence. There have been a few challenging days when the only person I could be totally open with was my journal.

I promise you that when you have an outlet to vent frustrations to, you will live more freely and be a happier person. Bottling up your feelings is a recipe for disaster, for when those thoughts eventually come to a head, the result could rob you of your health and happiness.

And it's not just the bad times that should be captured in your journal: fill it up with ideas and celebrations. Make its pages come alive to give you the strength to look at the future with courage!

Take Action

1. Buy a journal today. Make sure it's pretty to look at and easy to carry with you everywhere.
2. When you have aha moments, frustrating seasons, or events you struggle to understand, write in your journal.

Documenting little details of your everyday life becomes a celebration of who you are.

—Carolyn V. Hamilton

K Is for *Kind*

My favourite dictionary definition for the word *kind* as written in the Chambers Dictionary is "friendly, helpful, well-meaning, generous, benevolent or considerate." A kind person has a sympathetic attitude toward others. She is someone who has a willingness to do good or give pleasure to others. How nice is that? The world is so busy, and the hustle and bustle of daily life can make us totally oblivious to the needs of others. Still, I have yet to find a person who doesn't rise an inch and become better when treated well and made to feel important.

Choosing to be a kind person is inexpensive, but it has the effect of a million pounds. In December 2015, I tried a little experiment: I chose to give a gift every day. I really couldn't afford it, but I was buoyed up by the pleasure I knew it would give others at such a busy time. My array of gifts was as diverse as you can imagine, from a five-pound Starbucks voucher to articles of clothing to sometimes fairly substantial monetary amounts. I watched faces light up as recipients unwrapped the gifts. Even now, the feeling I got from that experience makes me smile.

Being kind doesn't have to involve money. You can offer a gift of time or even a smile. What

matters is that it is done with one goal in mind—
to make the other person feel better and, if I may
say, important!

Take Action

1. Whom can you show kindness today?

   _____

   _____

2. How will you express it?

   _____

   _____

   _____

A kind gesture can reach a wound that
only compassion can heal.

—Steve Maraboli

L Is for *Loyal*

Be loyal, be faithful, and be true to those you commit to as friends. In this journey called life, you will find people who stick with you through thick and thin and commit to helping you achieve all you set out to. Please do not be a person who enjoys such favours without giving back. Be that person who doesn't waver as you support the people and the causes you believe in.

Will there be times when you feel the need to decamp? Definitely! You will, however, build a strong character and an enviable reputation when you choose to remain on the side of those you have chosen to care for.

Be slow to fall into friendship, but when you are in, continue firm and constant.

—Socrates

M Is for *Manners*

Permit me to say that manners matter. Isn't it amazing that while the world thrives on the madness of being who you are and doing what you want, the higher echelons of society still celebrate traditional values of etiquette? Who has ever frowned at the golden words *please* and *thank you*? You are, however, sure to draw unwanted attention when those words are missing from your vocabulary. See why I insist that manners matter?

Take time to understand the society you live in, find out what the standards of etiquette are, and educate yourself in the practice of those standards at their highest level. In your daily living, practice using what you've learned, and before long, it will become second nature. Keep as your focus the salient prize of being cultured, and anticipate that otherwise impregnable doors will fling open.

I am not advocating for you to shelve your uniqueness and preferences; all I ask is that you know the right things to do and do those things when they are expected of you.

Take Action

1. Before this week ends, research how to set a formal table. Practice it, and treat yourself to a formal dinner where you've laid the table well.
2. Learn to say *please*, *thank you*, and *hello* in five widely spoken languages.

Good manners have much to do with the emotions. To make them ring true, one must feel them, not merely exhibit them.

—Amy Vanderbilt

N Is for *Nurture*

What are you nurtured by, and who is nurtured by you? The very physiological composition of a woman suggests the ability to create and care for what is around her; that's why she has a womb to carry her young and has breasts to feed and nurture them until they mature.

While growing up, I just didn't think I could nurture. I was a tomboy, shunning every so-called feminine responsibility and easily embracing the more traditionally masculine roles. I thrived on the adrenaline of quick results and was oftentimes irritated by what I considered to be the slow pace of my female friends.

As I write this, I can't help but think of hunters and farmers. Both are skilled in bringing food home from the fields, but the hunter gets food instantly while the farmer tills the land to grow the food over a period. I, like most achieving girls, would naturally prefer the hunter's speed to the drawn-out processes of the farmer, but one day I asked myself a question that changed my way of thinking: "What happens to the family of the hunter when he's no longer able to hunt?"

You see, the whole process of farming, to a large extent, ensures the provision of sustenance over a long period of time and continues to do so even after the farmer is long gone. Being a nurturer paves ways for you beyond today, and you must be intentional about moving from benefiting from those around you to nurturing them and helping them grow.

To nurture simply means to protect, preserve, and grow what is in your care. With this in mind, let the first question you ask yourself always be, "How can I help this person be better?" In answering that, you are stepping into the person you were created to be, and you will find strength to yourself be nurtured and benefit from your world even more.

Take Action

1. Make a list of your three closest friends.

   _____

   _____

   _____

2. How can you help them be better, and when will you start?

   _____

   _____

3. Write down two of your strengths.

    _____

    _____

    _____

4. Who could benefit from each strength?

    _____

    _____

The purpose of life is not to be happy. It is to be useful, to be honorable, to be compassionate, to have it make some difference that you have lived and lived well.

—Ralph Waldo Emerson

O Is for *Organised*

I consider organisation and orderliness to be two of my biggest strengths. Please understand the following:

- A scattered mind does not do anyone any good.
- A scattered mind causes stress.
- A scattered mind is not productive.
- A scattered mind is inefficient.

Give me a whole day, and I will still have things to say about a scattered mind.

It is common knowledge that organised people are more productive because their brains focus on getting work done rather than searching for what needs to be done. While I agree that some people are more gifted in this area, I promise you that being orderly is a choice and a skill that can be mastered.

Start with your wardrobe: decide to keep it tidy and organised for just one week, and soon you will be motivated to continue because you will have enjoyed the benefits of knowing where everything is.

Next move on to your daily tasks. Try writing out tomorrow's plan before going to bed tonight.

Does having a plan make a difference in how productive you are? I find that when I plan my day the night before, my brain seems to kick into execution mode in the morning. Instead of thinking of what to do, it goes straight into action. The benefit of this is that I save time in execution and am thus more productive.

Organising is what you do before you do something so that when you do it, it is not all mixed up.

—A. A. Milne

A place for everything, and everything in its place.

—Mrs. Beeton

P Is for *Pace*

Another favourite of mine is pacing. Sadly, in trying to become more significant, many people never reach the end of their race. They burn out and have their life cut out in their youth. While I am not an athlete and cannot lay claim to being sporty in any way, I do enjoy watching sports. I also know that there are different strategies for running a race, depending on the distance.

Life is like a long-distance race, and your task is to run it as best you can. Of course there will be ups and downs: sometimes you will feel squeezed out of your lane, the conditions you started off with may change; at times you will tire and want to give up, and occasionally you will have bursts of energy. What I have learned from watching races is that you need to decide on a strategy from the outset. Pace yourself based on what you know, take time to allow your body to find a rhythm, and then maintain that rhythm. So also in life, I encourage you to take time to rest amid the bursts of energy and peaks of success you are sure to enjoy.

My friends often laugh at me because I plan my breaks. This, I believe, is how nature designed life to be lived. If you don't believe me, find a farmer and ask about the effect of leaving a land fallow on the resultant productivity of that land. Apply this to your life, too! Time taken out to rest will result in more productivity.

Take Action

1. Make a list of tasks you need to achieve this month.
2. Plan your breaks! When will they be, and what will you do?

Small steps may appear unimpressive, but don't be deceived. They are the means by which perspectives are subtly altered, mountains are gradually scaled, and lives are drastically changed.

—Richelle E. Goodrich

Q Is for *Question*

In my desire to be the best version of me and optimise everyone in my world, one of my favourite things to do is to question my processes. I am constantly querying what I do, why I do it, and how I do it. I look for ways to make my processes better and more efficient. Just think—how can you be optimized when you do not know your current standing or capability?

A best practice to keep you growing is to question your processes. There's no point in going full throttle without looking back to take stock. A few pages ago, I talked about being organized, and questioning your processes is one of the keys to becoming organized. For any duty you carry out repeatedly, ask yourself if you have given it your best. For duties that cause you stress, ask yourself what you did wrong and what you did right. Once you've arrived at your answers, be bold enough to write them down and build a system around them.

I can't remember where I saw it, but the best definition of *system* I've seen was an acronym: Save Your Self Time, Energy & Money. Questioning, arriving at solutions, and developing a system around these solutions will definitely save you time, energy, and money in the long run.

Take Action

1. Pick a process that you constantly engage in (e.g., taking exams, going on school trips, or having guests).
2. Question the processes involved, and research better ways to do them.

There is only one corner of the universe you can be certain of improving, and that's your own self.

—Aldous Huxley

R Is for *Respect*

Most of my young life was spent in Western Nigeria, where being respectful is considered one of the best virtues anyone can possess. We attached titles to names, calling everyone Uncle or Aunty to show respect. We didn't dare to challenge an adult's opinion, let alone look one straight in the eyes, and when we greeted an elder, we curtsied to show reverence.

Looking back now, I must admit that some of these customs were perhaps a bit over the top. Having lived in the United Kingdom as well, I understand that the expression of respect differs from one culture to another. The universal truth about respect, however, is that you never lose out by being respectful. Try saying "Good day" to an elderly person on the street, and watch his or her face light up. You can't be too respectful, and it is better to give too much than too little.

More important is to make an effort to understand what respect means in the culture you live in. Then accord the people in your world the respect that is due every day. Respect is about more than making people feel good; it is a seed that comes back to you. You will find that as you become known as a respectful person, people will accord you the same.

Take Action

1. Where do you live, and what does respect mean in that culture?
2. For the next week, express respect in the highest form you can, especially to older people in your world.

Respect for ourselves guides our morals;
Respect for others guides our manners.

—Laurence Sterne

S Is for *Serve*

Some of the most respected people in our community are members of the armed forces. These men and women choose to serve their country, even unto death. The ability to give oneself to the service of another or in service to a cause has been proven to elongate life and give meaning to it.

Think of notable people like Mother Theresa, who chose to shun life's comforts for the opportunity to bring meaning, dignity, and focus to the lives of others. Think of the missionaries who went over to West Africa to improve living standards; think of Olympic athletes who proudly wear the colours of their countries and deny themselves in order to bring glory and repute to their countries.

Serving gives you a reason to wake up in the morning. When you are down or when hope is lost, you will find it easy to draw strength from the lives that hang on to your expression of service.

While you might not have the opportunity to travel thousands of miles and have your name on everyone's lips, you can make a decision to serve your local community. Ask yourself, "What needs to be done, and what help can I give?" Then, without batting an eyelid, realign your priorities and create time to lend a helping hand.

Draw inspiration from Morrie Boggart, who though diagnosed as terminally ill devotes himself to serving the needs of the homeless by knitting hats for them. According to him, this gives him strength for the next day.

As you serve the little needs of others, someone else will be inspired to serve the big needs that will make a difference in *your* life.

The best way to not feel hopeless is to get up and do something. Don't wait for good things to happen to you. If you go out and make some good things happen, you will fill the world with hope, you will fill yourself with hope.

—Barack Obama

T Is for *Thankful*

"Overcoming every problem begins with a thankful heart." And that, my dear, is one of the best lines I have ever heard. Thank you, Ricky and Cathy Ruso, for your 1994 song "A Thankful Heart." That line has kept me thankful.

Every morning when I wake up, I am unconsciously drawn to the problems going on in my life and around me: bills to pay, unaccomplished goals, friends to visit, and all that makes up our daily grind. Like most people, I have a tendency to start my day on a negative foot, thereby losing focus and falling short on productivity. What I find is that when I take time out to pause and reflect on my accomplishments, no matter how little, the problems fade into oblivion, and instead of starting my day downtrodden, I get the spark of optimism that gives my day a different vibe, making me more productive.

I watched *The Secret* a while ago and remember the reference to a "gratitude rock." The idea behind this rock is to help you celebrate what you have instead of focusing on what you want.

Did you know that focusing on recollecting things you are thankful for trains your brain to become more optimistic and have the can-do attitude that is an essential ingredient of living a significant life?

In the story of Adam and Eve, they had everything in the garden of Eden, except the "tree in the middle of the garden." Rather than celebrating, being thankful, and maximising all they had, they obsessed over what they *didn't* have, and that ultimately cost them a life in paradise.

Our brothers and sisters across the pond take a day out every November to celebrate Thanksgiving. While it might seem like a simple gesture, I encourage you to set aside the first ten minutes of your day to fill out a gratitude journal. Write about something you are grateful for from the previous day, and enjoy as your mind becomes more positive and you become happier!

Take Action

Buy yourself a gratitude journal and when you wake up in the morning, write in it one thing you are grateful for.

Thankfulness creates gratitude which generates contentment that causes peace.
—Todd Stocker

U Is for *Uniqueness*

The lines on your palm, the texture of your voice, and the features on your face are all unique to you. So unique, in fact, that a single strand of your hair can tell scientists who you—among the more than seven billion people on this earth— are. Doesn't that excite you? You are unique; you are special. There's only one of you!

What does your uniqueness offer other than the opportunity to stand out in the crowd? And what is the essence of standing out if it is not for notable strengths? This is the question I hope to answer by highlighting this quality. You must discover how your uniqueness strengthens your cause and helps you thrive.

In his book *Good to Great*, Jim Collins talks about how the hedgehog, using the simple principle of curling up when it senses impending danger, stays alive in the wild. Just imagine that tiny animal surviving where bigger ones fail to.

You must find out how your uniqueness feeds your strength and powers you to achieve your purpose. It's not just about being different; it's about that difference being leveraged as strength!

Take Action

Draw three triangles, and put one of your strengths in the middle of each. Then analyse them as shown in the diagram below. This will remind you of how to use your strength again in future.

How I will use it from today

Make the most of yourself...for that is all there is of you.

—Ralph Waldo Emerson

V Is for *Value*

If you have two diamonds of equal value and you wrap one in an old newspaper and set the other on fine black velvet, which one will draw attention? While the monetary value of the diamonds is the same, the presentation gives each a different *perceived* value.

For the world to respect your gift and who you are, you must place value on yourself. You must do everything you can to put your best foot forward. Before you step out of your house daily, ask yourself, "Is this the best way I can present myself today?" If the answer is no, go back indoors, and don't leave without giving yourself a thumbs up.

Remember, before you have the opportunity to speak, people make judgments. I am not asking you to become consumed with excessive adornments or to spend a fortune on clothes, as is the folly of many. All I ask is that you are proud of how you have *packaged* yourself.

On the flip side, do you realise that you might be undervaluing the people around you and are thus getting less than their best from them? If you look keenly at the people in your world, you will find the unique strengths that set them apart. While you work on yourself to have the best perceived value, become a master of searching out the rough diamonds around you and doing your bit to ensure that they are well packaged and presented. You will not only help develop their potential, but you also will benefit from all they have to offer.

Everyone enjoys being acknowledged and appreciated. Sometimes even the simplest act of gratitude can change someone's entire day. Take the time to recognize and value the people around you and appreciate those who make a difference in your lives.

—Roy T. Bennett

W Is for *Wisdom*

Wisdom is simply the right application of knowledge. Over the years, you have gained knowledge. This process started the first time you learned to suckle at your mother's breast. Then you learned to count, read, sing, dance, and even earn an income. In your season of learning, have you applied all you have learned? Perhaps a better way to ask that is, "Have you applied all you have learned to the best of your ability?" I have yet to meet anyone who answered both questions with a strong affirmative. And you are right to have doubts. Success is not just about gathering knowledge; it is also about using that knowledge wisely.

It is famed that the richest man who ever lived was also the wisest man ever—a certain King Solomon. Many have linked his propensity for wealth to his wisdom, and I also believe there is a strong link between success and wisdom.

The question now is, "How do I become a wiser person?" Start by following the steps below.

Take Action

1. Pray. This is simple but effective. Your mind has to feel gifted to be wise.
2. Hang around wise people. At the beginning, we looked at the seed becoming a plant. The farmer growing that plant could learn how to make the plant thrive by spending time with a successful farmer and learning from him.
3. When you have the opportunity to choose right, do it! As you practice being wise, you will become an expert at being wise.
4. Learn from past mistakes. Mistakes should never drag you down. Rather, they should teach you how not to behave, react, or speak.

The only true wisdom is in knowing you know nothing.
—Socrates

X Is for *Xenodochial*

Xenodochial is an adjective describing something—such as a person, place, or software application—that is friendly to strangers. *Xenos* is a Greek word for "strangers." According to the *Oxford English Dictionary*, the word *xenodochial* means "hospitable."

Besides sounding extremely intellectual when I use it, I love what this word brings to the table: it captures the essence of who you should be.

Nothing you do or promote should appear so foreign that it is irrelevant. Your personality, your views, and your inventions will be better accepted when you have done all you can to make them friendly towards those encountering them for the first time. It's a decision, I know, but it's one I never want you to take lightly. You are created for greatness, and your presentation should attract, not attack, the status quo. When you win people over through attraction, they stay with you longer and aid your cause.

Take Action

1. Reflect upon well-meaning actions that have been considered strange by people around you. Make a list of a few.
2. Is there any way your intention can be better presented or expressed?

Do not neglect to show hospitality to strangers, for by doing that some have entertained angels without knowing it.

—Hebrews 13: 2, Holy Bible (King James Version)

Y Is for *Youthful*

All I become and do today is about how my legacy benefits those coming behind me tomorrow. It's my #LegacyLiving. When Thomas Edison invented the light bulb, he wasn't just thinking about himself: he knew it would benefit you and me. The same goes for inventors of medicine, automobiles, and all the conveniences we enjoy today.

For me, all I engage in today is dictated on its effect on the next generation. But how can we reach the next generation if we are not relevant? Make an effort to be in the know with what young people are experiencing. I've had to understand social media, know the names of a few musicians, and be familiar with the shows that you, my children, watch so that I am not seen as the archaic mum but as someone who, through understanding where you are, is relevant and can give advice to you.

Think for a moment of a relay race. Imagine if the person passing the baton didn't make an effort to run to the recipient of the baton. The race would be lost—not because of skill, but because the gap was not closed.

My advice to you as you mature into adulthood is to stay youthful. Note that I didn't say to act young, as doing so will create the negative image of a wannabe.

Just be curious and show interest in what is coming up behind you, and you will be able to adequately pass on that baton.

There's nothing more contagious than the laughter of young children; it doesn't even have to matter what they're laughing about.

—Criss Jami

Z Is for *Zeal*

I can think of no better way to end this chapter than to scream: ZEAL! *Zeal*, according to the online 'Dictionary.com' is defined as "fervour for a person, cause, or object; eager desire or endeavour; enthusiastic diligence; ardour". It connotes intensity, passion, and all the attributes that you need to live the life I dream of for you.

I have written the twenty-five attributes above, but they will have little effect if you don't choose to apply them to your life with concentrated zeal! The attitude with which you embrace the twenty-five cornerstones above will determine the results you get, and I sure hope it is an attitude of zeal.

Take Action

1. Review the *A* to *Z* list again.
2. Write out three areas you most want to develop.

   _____
   _____
   _____

3. Who can help you with these three?

4. Schedule a meeting or phone call with that person, and put a plan in place.

Perfection is pure action that comes with zeal to excel.

—Vikrmn, Corpkshetra

To review, our *A* to *Z* are as follows:

A is for *AFFIRMATION*

B is for *BELIEF*

C is for *COMMUNICATION*

D is for *DRIVE*

E is for *EXCELLENCE*

F is for *FUN*

G is for *GOALS*

H is for *HEALTH*

I is for *INVEST*

J is for *JOURNAL*

K is for *KIND*

L is for *LOYAL*

M is for *MANNERS*

N is for *NURTURE*

O is for *ORGANISED*

P is for *PACE YOURSELF*

Q is for *QUESTION YOUR PROCESSES*

R is for *RESPECT*

S is for *SERVE*

T is for *THANKFUL*

U is for *UNIQUENESS*

V is for *VALUE*

W is for *WISDOM*

X is for *XENODOCHIAL*

Y is for *YOUTHFUL*

Z is for *ZEAL*

In the next chapter, I will be tackling one key factor that plays a role in who you become, and it's the subject of your life partner. I am not a relationship expert, but I have been married for a while now, and I know where I made mistakes and what I did right. I hope my experience with the topic provides nuggets of wisdom that serve as a guide as you begin. I have also asked my good friend to co-write that section with me, as I want you to have a balanced view. It's not all about him, but—believe me—he matters!

> *We are a sum total of what we have learned from all who have taught us, both great and small.*
>
> - Myles Munroe

PART 3

A Key Area: Relationships

A Key Area: Relationships
This will be a nurturer, not a pest.

Our journey continues with a chapter that almost didn't make it to this book—the relationship chapter! You may be wondering why I changed my mind. Well, it's pretty simple. On my journey, I have met many women who completely gave up on their dreams and their journey of significance because they lacked support from people they'd built relationships with. Relationships should be one of the nurturing elements referred to in part 1, but for some they become the pest or parasite that drains and derails.

There are lots of relationships we can talk about—relationships with your siblings, friends, colleagues, and so on—but to me the big one is the marital relationship, and that will be the focus for the rest of the chapter. As important as it is to learn useful attitudes and find your purpose, there is no point to doing so if what you have learned ends up crushed and destroyed by the man you choose to marry.

There are two perspectives in the interpretation of relationships—the male perspective and the female perspective. To ensure you get a balanced view, I have asked my friend Folarin (Flo) Falayi to co-write this chapter. Folarin is a relationship and leadership expert based in the United States. I have known him for over twenty-five years, and I admire his take on relationship matters, so you are getting a real treat. My thoughts and motherly advice are summed up under "Her Words" while Folarin's section is called "His Words." My prayer is that as you read through the next few pages, you will find enough material to begin your journey and the wisdom to make the right choices.

Her Words

The best way to boost your marital relationship is to enter into it assuming it is a lifetime commitment. This attitude will shape your decisions and the way you navigate the marriage.

Would you invest a lot of money in developing a house that you were renting for a short period of time? Probably not! Any investment you make or structure you build in that property will be decided upon based on how long you intend to stay there and limited by the fact that it doesn't belong to you. If, on the other hand, you buy a property and know it's yours for as long as you want to have it, you will likely put together a plan to develop it to be the best it can be.

Marriage is similar. Choosing to treat it like a "forever adventure" shapes every decision you make, before or after you commit to it. Like a house buyer, you will experience two main phases: before the purchase and after the purchase.

If the "before" phase is done properly, with the right questions asked, you will find the alterations, adjustments, and refurbishments in the "after" phase to be minimal. Hey, I know people buy property with the intention of putting their mark on it and doing a lot of work on it, but in this case, we'll just keep this simple and assume that the goal is to live with minimal adjustments to the property and focus on building as a way to enhance, not correct.

Before Committing

Let's have some fun and assume the role of a house buyer together. Some of the questions we may ask include the following:

1. What do I like about this house?
2. Does it meet my requirements today?
3. How easily can I tailor it to meet future needs of expansion?
4. Is it structurally sound and secure?

5. Where is it located, and what sort of lifestyle can I expect based on the area it is located in?
6. Is the location susceptible to flooding? If yes, do I like it enough to commit to the expense?
7. How close is it to my workplace? Do I like it enough to make the long commute?

The list could go on and on. I will not bore you by drawing a line-by-line analogy of the questions as they relate to choosing a future partner; you have probably started making comparisons in your mind already. But I do have a few questions that you could ask yourself about a future spouse:

1. What do I love about him that cannot change?

Many start out loving only physical characteristics. I laugh out loud as I write that line because, sadly, these are the first to change. Luckily my husband has not changed much physically, so this is in no way a reference to him. While he can still fit into his wedding suit, I have advanced my dress sizes a few times!

Can you imagine if my attraction to my husband had been based on changeable characteristics? I would have lost staying power as soon as I no longer saw these qualities in him. I recommend you make your "I Love Him Because" list based on innate characteristics like the following:

a. integrity
b. manner of reasoning
c. work ethic
d. life philosophies

These to me are as important as the structure of the house, which—no matter how outwardly pretty the house looks—should never be compromised. If the house is structurally shaky, marriage will not change it; it will only highlight these failings, and the house will collapse in very little time.

2. What background does he come from, and how does it complement mine?

In an earlier chapter, I talked about how perspectives form the basis of interpretation and, consequently, behaviour. As the old adage says, "The apple doesn't fall far from its tree." There is a 99.9 percent chance that his background will affect him. Many men will be an exact replica of their dads. In fact, their fathers are imprinted in their subconscious minds, and this comes into play in decision making in later years. If a man had a father who was authoritative in his approach, and made all the decisions, he will probably adopt this leadership style too and be authoritative in his approach. Likewise, the influence of his mother. So assuming he had a stay-at-home mum and loved this, he will most likely never accept a high-flying career woman. If, on the other hand, he felt that his mum's staying at home deprived him of additional pleasures, he will be unable to accept a wife who chooses to stay home. I hope this opens up a new dimension to the background question. Realise it is the interpretation of his background that shapes future behavioural patterns. Take time to question what you are unsure of, and allow this to inform the decisions you make.

3. What did I dislike about my parents while growing up?

This is an important question that many try to ignore. In a bid to move on from the scars of our past, we mask the things that we hated, checking them off as being okay, but sadly we react to them negatively when they happen. Let me make this clearer with an example. Assume your father never went to sports day. Your mother might have been fine with this behaviour, but it made your heart ache every time it happened. If this mattered to you when you were a child, it will matter still when you have children and your husband refuses to go along with you. Fine as it might have been for your mum, you don't have to accept it as a norm. And if it is important to you, it's worth bringing up and deciding on before you commit to a spouse.

4. How does he treat his mum and the women in his life?

To him, you are a woman, and how he treats you will not be far off from how he treats and has treated other women. Does he value what you bring to the table, or does he see it as a target to exceed? Choose a spouse who thinks the world of you, values what makes you unique as a woman, and constantly builds you up without comparing your strengths to his abilities. He must be confident enough to let you fly without feeling threatened.

5. What are his plans for the future?

Be bold enough to discuss this *before* committing. Don't hide your agenda with the guise of buying him over after marriage, as this hardly works and instead causes friction. Resolve differences of opinions on how many children to have, where to live, how much influence extended family will have, and as much as you can think of before marriage. You might not start out with the same ideas, but talking about these issues and reaching an agreement will set benchmarks for the future.

6. How does he argue or resolve conflict?

I have heard couples boast about how alike they are and how they never disagree or argue. This raises a red flag for me immediately, as I believe it is impossible to live together for so long without having disagreements. It's therefore good practice to rehearse this before committing to marriage. Choose a spouse who sees disagreements as a way to fashion a joint agreement. Avoid men who stifle your opinion and stop you from expressing your mind. You can't be silent forever, and if you don't feel empowered to speak your mind, you will feel the need to resort to manipulative ways to execute your plans. Being manipulative is the quickest way to break trust, an integral part of any marriage.

7. What is his view of life?

Does he have a light-hearted nature and approach life with positivity and humour, or is he overly suspicious, pessimistic, and unable to relax? Life is sure to throw challenges your way, and the last thing you want is to have a persistently negative person in your court. Choose a man who smiles positively at the future, is constantly full of hope, and sees good where others don't.

The list of questions above is not comprehensive, but it is a good place to start. Once you have made your decision on the "right guy," your journey begins. Your aim should be to complete him, not compete with him. In completing him, seek out his best qualities, and remind him constantly of why he is special, why you would choose him again and again, and why he is the best person for you. Such behaviour will boost his confidence, make him feel valued, and give him a place of respite in difficult situations. Many live life feeling alone and are only a shadow of what they could be. When your spouse is fulfilled and feels he owes this to you, he is likely to repay the favour and give you the opportunity to be fulfilled, too.

In marriage, our focus shifts from what we can get to what we can give, for in giving we get much more than we could ever have bargained for.

His Words
(written by Flo Falayi, Ph.D)

Dear Daughter,

I hope you read this letter somewhere quiet; I hope you are alone, sitting down, and imagining each sentence as an introduction to a chapter because that's exactly how I envisage each one to be—a reflective passage to further conversation. I hope you will read this often as I intend to be direct, upfront and frank.

Marriage is hard work. Relationships are difficult and challenging. The challenge with relationships is that due to their complicated nature and complexity, they are often painted with broad brushstrokes. Sadly, many clichés and opinions are not applicable, and when we do decide to rationalise our thinking on relationships, we complicate simple things by overthinking or overanalysing due to ignorance or limited information. That is one trap you must avoid.

As you transition from your younger years into adulthood, prepare for the onslaught of questions on relationships. It would be wise to be ready even if you are not ready. Does this sound confusing? Don't worry, it will become clearer.

As you grow older, be ready for questions and concerns from those who love you. Many of these questions will centre on what you like, who you like, and other cultural nuances and feedback. Listen intently - be thankful for these intrusions, especially at family gatherings, events, and parties. Embrace the process, and enjoy it if you can. I have seen it play out over and over, and I hear many say in retrospect that their lack of attention was a watershed moment.

Heartbreaks

Relationships are fun, amazing ways to learn more about yourself. As you go through this stage, you will stumble and make some mistakes. My heart goes out to you because while I would like to help you, it is probably best I step back and let your heart develop the resilience you will need to succeed in relationships. I have experienced a few heartbreaks. They are tough but very good for your heart.

Compatibility

Compatibility matters when it comes to who you eventually settle down with, so perform the due diligence necessary to ensure you see things similarly. It's one thing to stop saying the wrong things but you've got to start saying the right things. If you are not compatible, don't force it. Can two work together if they are not in agreement? Absolutely not.

Never stop being yourself

In relationships, you will be tempted to deny your true self. Don't do that. You will be pressured to compromise your stance and standards. Do not yield to those pressures. Be true to yourself and who you were raised to be.

Ask questions

If there is one thing I can advise you to do, it is to get comfortable asking questions. Asking questions is the simplest and most effective method of learning and discovering. Understand this, dearest one – the right questions can be surgical. I wish I had developed the knack for asking questions a lot earlier in life; in retrospect, I realise that by not asking questions, I was unintentionally limiting the possibilities and opportunities around me. Do not let the same happen to you.

When you ask questions, be aware of the types of questions you are asking. Try to avoid closed questions, which generally elicit *yes* or *no* answers. Instead, ask open-ended questions. These open up a wide range of opportunities and possibilities and lead to an elaboration of issues and concerns.

Additionally, you should employ the two-question rule, which means to follow a question with another question—one that probes for deeper understanding. In general, the key to discovery is in asking questions and paying close attention to the subtle nuances and phrases in the responses.

Give it time and trust your spirit

If you are patient, love will find you. And if you are reflective and patient enough, true love will emerge. I know how time works and how, in time, perspectives are fully developed. The same is applicable here. I hope you will allow time to play a distinct role in your relationship because in time you will see things blossom. Time has the amazing ability to confirm and reveal intentions. One of my favourite scriptures highlights the power of quiet confidence, and I agree that there is great strength in solitude, reflection, and honesty.

Final Words on This Subject
I hope you got a good picture from the two perspectives above. My letter is now concluded, and all I have left to pass on to you in the last chapter are a few acronyms I wrote in the past. They summarise all I've discussed and give you the opportunity to discover yourself as you begin your own journey. I have no doubt in my mind that you are now equipped to take the next steps, and I want you to remember that I am cheering you on!

Few people who marry plan for their marriages to fail, but neither do they specifically plan for success.

—Myles Munroe

PART 4

My Acronyms

I have become known as the Acronym Queen. I have always loved acronyms; they were the way I learned to memorise difficult concepts in school, for I found it easier to remember one word that summarised an idea than to remember long sentences.

1. **I CAN**
   This was the very first acronym I wrote, and as you can imagine, it holds an important place in my heart. It summarises what I consider the path to achieving anything you desire.

   I - I (my individuality and uniqueness)
   C - Commitment
   A - Affirmation
   N - Never giving up

2. **QUIZ**
   I am a systematic person. I believe that most things can be achieved more easily if you take the time to build a system around them.

   Q—Question your processes.
   U—Understand your uniqueness.
   I—Imitate a successful person.
   Z—Zero in on what works.

3. **GROW**

In this series, I used the analogy of conception to birth as a step-by-step guide to going from idea to realization.

G—Get pregnant with your goals.
R—Rid yourself of excesses.
O—Observe and align.
W—Work to push the baby out.

4. **LIVE**

I love all my acronyms; however, some hold more meaning than others. If there is one acronym that sums up who I am and what I believe, it's this one.

L—Learn consistently.
I—Invest in yourself.
V—Value people around you.
E—Excel at whatever you do.

5. **ABC**

   I wasn't born in England, and while working my nine-to-five, I happened to be the only black person in my office. I realised that there were set rules of etiquette that everyone knew. As soon as I could afford it, I went to etiquette school for a week, and this was my key learning.

   A—Appearance: you are judged by this.
   B—Behaviour: you are measured by this.
   C—Communication: shows how you think.

6. **FLY**

   Birds fly. They defy gravity, and this endears them to us. In this series, I ask, "What gives me wings? What makes me fly?"

   F—Friends that encourage you
   L—Loving what you do
   Y—Why: understanding your why

7. **STAR**

What gives me star quality? What makes me stand out? What gives me an edge over my peers? In this series, I discuss what I've found to give me star quality.

S—Service
T—Thankfulness
A—Advancing daily
R—Respect for others

8. **TOP**

This acronym came to me as I contemplated my career and how I had been blessed to excel and be one of the top performers for so long.

T—Tenacity
O—Orderliness
P—Pacing

9. **WAY**

How do you ensure that your brain is not cluttered with ideas? How do you ensure that you are in control of your thoughts and actions? Find a way!

W—Write: have a notebook to scribble things down when you think of them.
A—Act: take the next step.
Y—Yet: a hope that what is not evident today may well be tomorrow's reality

10. **GAP**

This acronym was inspired by my desire to bridge the gap and make the world a better place because I'm in it.

G—Gratitude for all I enjoy
A—Amplifying my gifts and talents
P—Passing it on (the inspiration for this book)

11. USE

In December 2015, I volunteered as a chorister in my church. I was shocked to find that I struggled to remember the lines. Considering I used to remember the IP addresses of my servers and sixteen-digit card numbers, this was a big concern. That experience inspired USE it.

U—Understand
S—Study
E—Experiment

12. WAIT

This acronym was inspired by the rags-to-riches story of Olajumoke Orisaguna. It contains my advice on what to do while you wait.

W—Work harder.
A—Assist others.
I—Improve daily.
T—Take chances.

13. DREAMS

In preparation for my first MAP (Motivate, Adorn, Prepare) workshop, which was all about finding and living your dreams, I sought to summarise what it means to dream.

Desire **R**esults,
Expect **A**ntagonism, but
Maintain **S**elf-belief!

14. CROP

In preparation for another first—the launch of my online school—I wrote this acronym to explain how to bring any idea to fruition.

C—Create a list.
R—Rank the items on the list.
O—Optimise the items.
P—Plan your strategy.

15. PERK

In continuation of my teaching on getting organised, I wrote this acronym to show how to ensure you are constantly achieving the set objectives from the plans you put in place.

P—Plan
E—Execute
R—Review
K—Keep

16. WIN

At the end of the 2016 Rio Olympics, I was so impressed by the athletes that I wrote an acronym to summarise my thoughts on what makes them so successful.

W—Work hard.
I—Inspire others.
N—Never give up.

17. SPARK

It's the start of 2017, and the fireworks display (a revelation of beauty) reminds me that most fires start with a spark. This acronym discusses how to "make it happen" in your life.

S—Set your goal(s).
P—Put a plan in place.
A—Adjust your attitude.
R—Review constantly.
K—Keep a gratitude journal.

18. BATON

My inspiration for writing this book is to ensure I pass on all I have learnt, at the right time and in the best possible way. I drew inspiration from relay races, hence the reference to the baton. Here's what we need to pass on:

B - Belief
A - Attitudes
T - Trust
O - Optimism
N – Nurturing

So there you have it—my collection of acronyms to date. Please use these to enhance your life, but as with everything else in this book, do not use them publicly or in written material without prior consent from me.

Have a truly awesome time becoming the best version of you!

Always do your best in whatever you do; set goals and seek challenges; become a role model for those coming behind you; and always have God in your heart.

—Charles F. Bolden

CONNECT WITH 'FLO FALAYI

'Flo Falayi, Ph.D. is The Hybrid Leader™.
An American Born, British Educated and Nigerian
Raised Leadership & Organizational Development
Consultant, International Speaker, Pastor, Social
Entrepreneur and Radio Host.
He is extremely passionate about raising and sustaining
global leaders, empowering and enabling leaders and
organizations to maximize their most valuable
resources in a very competitive and increasing diverse
global economy.
Visit his website to find out more about his work.
www.relationshipsdomatter.com

CONNECT WITH DOYIN

Doyin Olorunfemi is a business woman, author and
motivational speaker who runs yearly **MAP** (**Motivate
Adorn Prepare**) workshops in London for women
every year in June. The purpose of these workshops is
not only to give women an opportunity to become
better versions of themselves, but to empower them to
'pass it on' to the next generation.

Doyin has a YouTube channel called: *'Minute
Motivation with Doyin'*, where she uses acronyms as an
effective means of passing on life lessons.
Website - www.doyin.co.uk
Twitter - @MinMotivation
Facebook – facebook.com/minutemotivation

20835465R00062

Printed in Great Britain
by Amazon